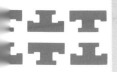

CONTENTS

Mmm! Food glorious food

There is a song that starts 'Food glorious food'. It comes from a famous musical called 'Oliver' where a little boy asks for more food because he is hungry. It would be awful to feel really hungry – to be starving. One of the things all animals must have – and that includes humans – is food.

Even though you are never starving is there something you really love to eat? Ice-cream, perhaps – or sausages? If you could ask for more of any food what would it be?

Food comes in many colours, shapes and sizes. Some food we *suck* – like sweets. Some we have to *lick* like ice-lollies. What sorts of food do we chew or bite?

Some food has very funny names. Is Shepherds' Pie really made from shepherds? What about Welsh Rabbit, Hot Cross Buns and Bangers and Mash?

CHILDREN'S LIBRARY

Food

nall

Series Consultant:
David Marshall
Rocks Park School

Technology Consultant:
David Jukes
Department of Food Science and Technology,
Reading University

Editor: Caroline Thomas
Designer: Ewing Paddock
Picture Research: Elizabeth Loving
Production: Ken Holt

Illustrators: Paul Cooper 6, 12-13, 14-15, 23, 24, 25,
    26, 27, 28-29
Helen Herbert 7, 16-17
Kate Rogers 6-7, 8-9, 18-19

Photographs:
Brian and Cherry Alexander 22
Ardea 17
Robert Harding 20 (right)
Hutchison Library 12, 13
NASA 16
OXFAM 11 (bottom)
Save the Children Fund 11 (top)
Science Photo Library 18 (all) 20 (left) 21 (left)
ZEFA 19, 21 (right), 23, 27

A MACDONALD BOOK

© Macdonald & Co (Publishers) Ltd 1987

First published in Great Britain in 1987 by
Macdonald & Co (Publishers) Ltd
London & Sydney
A BPCC plc Company

ISBN 0 356 13226 9

Printed and bound in Great Britain by
William Clowes Limited, Beccles and London

Macdonald & Co (Publishers) Ltd
Greater London House, Hampstead Road
London NW1 7QX

British Library Cataloguing in Publication Data
Marshall, David, *1945–*
    Food.—(My first technology library).
    1. Food—Juvenile literature
    I. Title   II. Series
    641.3   TX355
    ISBN 0-356-13226-9

How to use this book

First, look at the contents page opposite. Read the list to see if it includes the subject you want. The list tells you what each page is about, and you can find the page with information you need.

In the book, some words are **darker** than the others. These are harder words. Sometimes there is a picture to explain the word. For example, the word **trawler** appears on page 12 and there is a picture of it on page 13. Other words are explained in the word list on page 31.

On page 28 you will find a technology project. This project gives you lots of ideas and starting points for discovering technology for yourself.

**Calcium
Protein
Vitamin D
Fat**

Vitamin C

**Carbohydrate
Fat
Vitamin C**

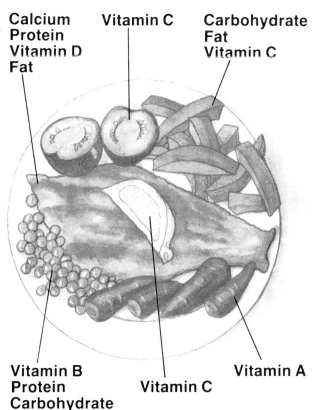

**Vitamin B
Protein
Carbohydrate**

Vitamin C

Vitamin A

We eat food not only to stop us feeling hungry but also to keep us healthy. Food contains substances that give us energy and keep us warm which are called carbohydrates and fats. Carbohydrates are in foods like bread, potatoes and sugar. Fats are in foods like milk and butter. There are other things called **proteins** that help us to grow and repair our bodies. We only need small amounts of minerals and vitamins but they are important too. There are about 17 of them and they each do a different job. For instance, you need vitamin A for good eyesight and the mineral calcium keeps your teeth and bones strong. We must eat the right amounts of all these things to keep us healthy and strong.

Coke and chapattis!

Have you ever been to a '**fast-food**' restaurant like Macdonalds? If so you know how quickly the food is ready for you. It probably takes American children longer to eat their meal than make it! It might be a hot dog, coleslaw and chips, followed by ice-cream sundae and coke to drink.

If you lived in India your evening meal might be: a dhal (lentil stew), chapattis (flat bread), chutney, vegetable curry, a raita (yoghurt salad) and rice. It would have taken about 3 hours to prepare and cook.

American meal

Natural food is food that is cooked simply and has no **artificial** chemicals or flavouring. The Indian meal is like that. It also has no meat in it. There is a lot of protein in meat, but there is protein in some vegetables too.

What goes into the sausage in the hot dog? Only about half of it will be meat! And probably not very good meat either. Because meat can be ground down into very tiny pieces any tough stringy meat will do. The rest of the sausage is cereal, **seasoning** and water. There is almost as much cereal in a hot dog as in the chapattis which are made from wheat flour! Cereal means any sort of grain, like rice, or oats – not just breakfast food.

Hardly anyone knows how Coca-Cola gets its flavour – it is a secret recipe. It does contain a great force of carbon dioxide – that is what makes it so fizzy.

Many years ago ice-cream was made from iced cream! Today most ice-creams are made from vegetable oils with colours and flavours added. It looks like frozen cream and tastes like it – but it isn't! And it's much cheaper to make and sell.

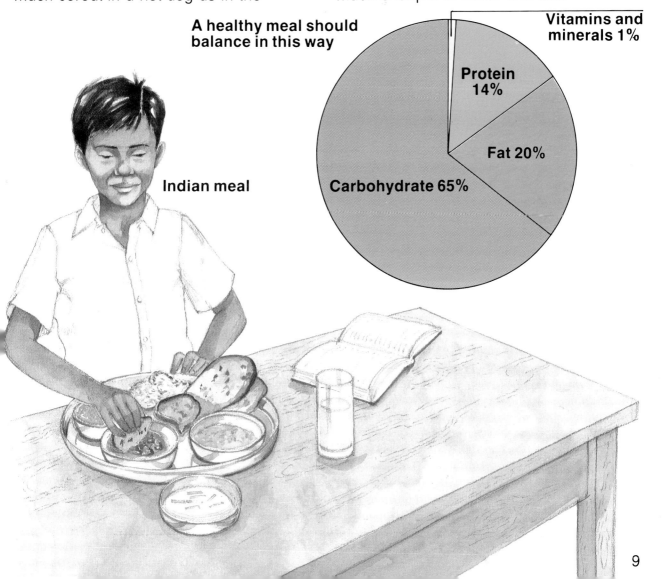

A healthy meal should balance in this way

Vitamins and minerals 1%

Protein 14%

Fat 20%

Carbohydrate 65%

Indian meal

A bowl of wheat, please

Ben had a very bad day last week. He woke up late and in the rush he burnt the toast. There wasn't the time to make more so he went without. The school lunch was fish pie, brussel sprouts, potatoes and rice pudding. Ben didn't like any of it, although it would have been good for him, so he had some potato and left the rest. Football practice made him late home and his parents had already gone out. He couldn't be bothered to get his own tea and when his mum got in she was cross with him and sent him straight to bed with a glass of milk. Ben sulked and refused to drink it. He went to sleep hungry – but that was his choice.

Small water pumps and big watering systems are needed i▮ poor countries

The Need For Water

Poor irrigation – lack of water – is the biggest handicap to giving everyone the food they need. In the year 1900 just 20 million acres, (8 million hectares), of the world's arable land was irrigated. By 1970 that figure had grown to 460 million acres, (180 million hectares). But we still need more. In Bangladesh 1 million pumps are needed to give everyone water – there are only 40,000 new ones each year.

On the same day as Ben was having his problems, Bali woke up in his little African village. There was no food for his breakfast, just a drink of water. For his lunch he queued up to be given a bowl of wheat – no water. This was much better than a few weeks before when, like everyone else, he had no food at all. This was his only meal. He was glad to have some more water though. Bali had no choice. He too went to bed hungry. Just like every other day of his life. But he was glad he was no longer starving. In fact he thought he was lucky to get so much!

Bob Geldof and Live Aid have shown how much work has to be done to help people who are starving. First of all they must be given food to keep them alive. Then new farm machinery must be bought for them and the best farming methods taught to them to make sure they never starve again. This is called long-term planning.

Hunting and catching food

Ever since time began, animals have hunted for their food, and people have hunted animals for the same reason. Before people knew how to write they drew pictures on cave walls showing their great hunters in action. The pictures show men using spears and clubs to catch and kill their food. Nowadays hunters use guns and traps to catch animals. Not all hunted food is big and dangerous. Australian **Aborigines** love eating witchetty grubs – which look a bit like maggots! You don't need a gun to trap those!

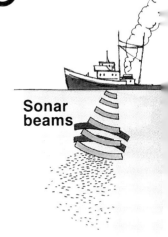

Sonar beams

Australian holding a witchetty grub

We can buy our meat in shops and we don't have to think about hunting it or killing it. There are animals bred on farms for us to eat but many people in the world still have to catch and hunt their food. If you lived in parts of India, Africa, South America or Australia you might have to hunt and kill your breakfast every day.

Perhaps the bravest men who get our food for us are the sea fishermen who go out in stormy weather worse than we can imagine. Some boats are called **trawlers** – they drag a huge net like a bag over the sea bed – trapping the fish as they go along. Others use **Seine fishing** – they close a net around fish in a giant circle.

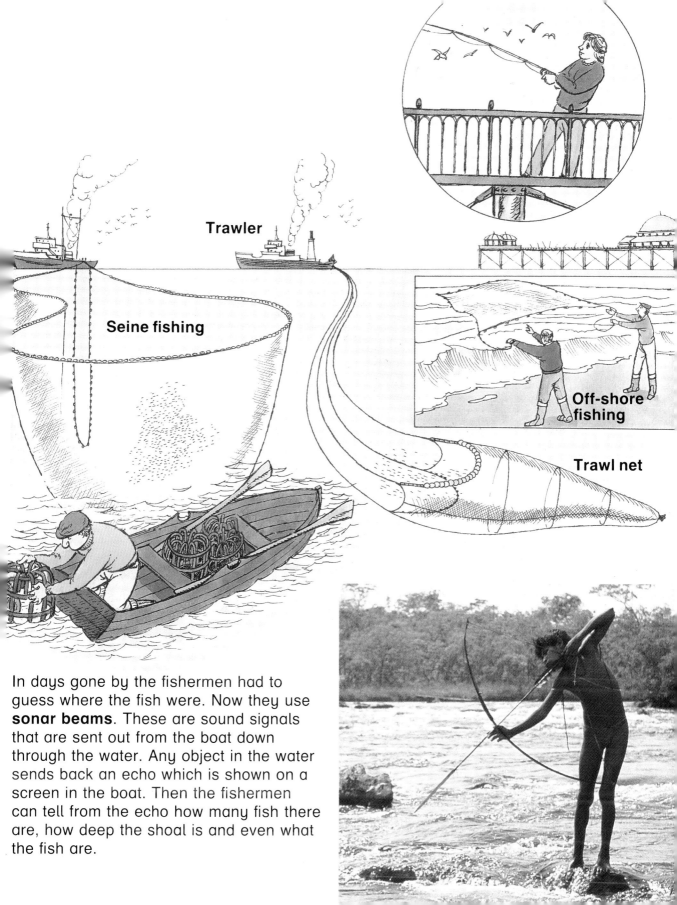

Trawler

Seine fishing

Off-shore fishing

Trawl net

In days gone by the fishermen had to guess where the fish were. Now they use **sonar beams**. These are sound signals that are sent out from the boat down through the water. Any object in the water sends back an echo which is shown on a screen in the boat. Then the fishermen can tell from the echo how many fish there are, how deep the shoal is and even what the fish are.

Rearing and growing food

Early people didn't bother to breed animals or plant seeds for themselves but just took what was there already and then moved on. Gradually people realised that they could keep animals for the food they gave and that they could plant and grow crops. They became farmers. Perhaps the most important way of getting food had arrived.

A few years ago every cow was milked by hand. It was a slow, tiring job. Nowadays, most farms have milking machines which do the job in no time at all.

Free Range
90p

In the olden days, people threw the seed onto a field by hand, walking up and down to cover the whole area. Today the farmer sits in the cab of a modern tractor that is pulling the **seed drill**. It is quicker and less tiring and more efficient too.

In order to produce eggs as cheaply as possible many farmers have set up 'factory farms'. Thousands of hens are kept in little cages inside big sheds. They are given just the right amount of food every day – the food supply is controlled by computer. The hens never go out – they just lay eggs. This saves space on the farm and the hens lay more eggs, which can be sold more cheaply, but the animals are kept in horrible conditions. Pigs and cows can be reared in the same way too. The eggs and meat are cheaper but people say they are less tasty these days, and many people aren't happy about treating animals so badly.

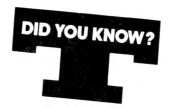

DID YOU KNOW?

A Small Mistake

We have to eat food to be healthy and strong. Popeye the Sailor is supposed to be strong because of all the spinach he eats. But this is a mistake! In 1870 a list of the best foods was published and someone put a decimal point in the wrong place and spinach seemed to be ten times richer in iron than any other food! In fact spinach contains oxalic acid and too much would make you ill.

FARM FRESH
60ᵖ

Making food

Although we hope there will always be enough food there are times when new foods have to be found to replace old ones. Between 1850 and 1870 the **population** of Europe nearly doubled. Some food, like butter became very scarce. A Frenchman developed margarine – the first really invented food. He mixed beef fat with dried milk. First it was advertised as being no different from butter to persuade people to buy it. Now it has been discovered that too much butter is bad for you, people buy margarine because they think it is different and will be better for them! These days margarine is made from vegetable oil.

Soya beans

Soya mince

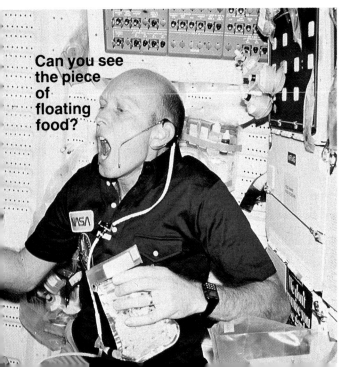

Can you see the piece of floating food?

Astronauts need special methods to be invented to help them enjoy their meals. In weightless conditions ordinary food like peas would float all over the room and water would roll up into a ball. In the early days of space travel astronauts sucked their food from a tube but these days scientists are finding ways to make their food more interesting to eat.

Would you like to eat krill?

Soya beans contain a lot of protein and they are cheap to grow, over 90 million tons are produced every year. The only trouble is they don't taste very nice! But scientists add different flavours to solve that problem. Now they can make a whole meal from soya – soya meat, soya gravy and soya cheese – all tasting different.

Japanese fishermen have caught so many fish that there are hardly any left in the seas around Japan. Now they are trying to persuade people to eat krill – a tiny creature with a lot of protein. There are huge shoals of krill, and there is enough krill in one shoal to give all 226 million Americans 45 kg each. The problem is that krill only live in the very cold and dangerous Antarctic ocean.

Soya sausages

Soya Oil

Jameson's Soya Flour

Margarine

SUNBURST Margarine

Good food not bad

There are millions of tiny creatures living all around us. They are so small we usually can't see them at all. When many of them collect together we can see them. Mould on an old orange is made out of thousands of these creatures. They feed off our food and make it go bad – like when milk turns sour. They grow very fast and then split to make two creatures. These split again, and again, and so their numbers grow very quickly. The more there are, the worse the food will taste and it may make you very sick. That is why if you leave food around for a long time it will go off, because these creatures have grown on the food.

Flies leave germs behind

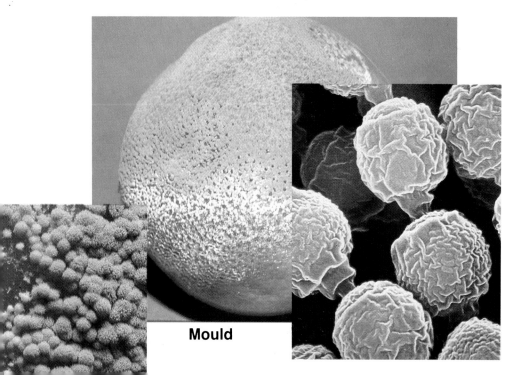

Mould

A canning factory must be extra clean!

We call these creatures micro-organisms. They are everywhere – in the air, on your hands, on furniture. Too many of them make us sick but washing will remove them. That is why your parents try to keep the kitchen clean and tell you to wash your hands. If you eat with dirty hands you put them in your mouth.

Keeping food cool slows down the growth of micro-organisms, which is why milk stays fresh longer in the fridge. Freezing stops the micro-organisms growing altogether – until they are defrosted. Cooking foods kills them as well. Factories seal foods like beans in a tin then cook the tin. The micro-organisms inside are killed and no more can get in.

Like us, micro-organisms need water to live so one way to stop them growing is to dry the food. You can get soup and pot noodles like this. When you want to eat them you add hot water and stir.

Food that has been dried or tinned won't go off because the micro-organism can't grow. It will last on a shelf for a long time – tinned food almost forever.

These germs can end up in our mouths

On the shelf

When you go into a supermarket all the food you need is already weighed and packed in boxes, packets or jars. Even vegetables like carrots are in sealed plastic packs to keep them fresh longer. It's easier for shops if every carrot is the same size – and that is how they are grown thanks to scientists! The box the food is in has a date stamped on it to show if it is still fresh enough to eat, and all the ingredients are there as well so you can see exactly what you are eating, if you can understand what it says! Look at the first four things listed in Instant Whip:

sucrose,   modified starch
dextrose, disodiumorthophosphate.

What do your carrots look like when you buy them?

The date on the food can often be a long way in the future. Scientists have made it possible to preserve food for a very long time. It makes life easier for shops and customers if they don't have to buy fresh food every day.

Often there are extra things in the food – known as **additives** – to keep the food fresh and make it look nicer. There are many substances allowed. Most of them have code numbers beginning with the letter E, like E217, which is propyl 4-hydroxybenzoate sodium salt!

Some of the additives are to make the food look nicer. We only like eating food that looks **appetising**. Most of us like our peas bright green and our raspberry jam a dark red. One manufacturer took all the added colouring out of his foods and his sales dropped by half! But the foods tasted just the same. He put the artificial colouring back but it was two years before he sold as much as before.

What do these E numbers stand for?

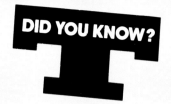

DID YOU KNOW?

Modern Ingredients

Can you work out what you would be eating from this list of ingredients? The answer is at the bottom of the page:

Monosodium glutamate
salt, chicken fat
dehydrated chicken
wheaten base, sugar
onion powder
hydrolized vegetable protein
dried parsley
ground white pepper
ground turmeric

AND TOMATO FLAVOUR SAUCE AND A SACHET OF TOMATO SAUCE

Ingredients: Wheatflour, Vegetable Oil with Antioxidants (E320, E321), Cheese & Tomato Flavour [Flavour Enhancer (621), Flavouring, Colours (E102, E110, E124, 154), Acidity Regulators (E262, E331), Acetic Acid, Citric Acid, Artificial Sweetener (Saccharin)], Maltodextrin, Salt, Tomato, Sweetcorn, Chives, Preservative (E220), Sachet: Tomato Sauce.

Chicken Noodle Soup Mix

A freezer full

Many years ago rich people would get their servants to cut huge blocks of ice from frozen lakes in winter. These would be packed into underground rooms or caves where the sun never shone. Then food could be stored there even in summer. These were known as ice-houses and were the first freezers.

There are some foods that we simply could not have if we couldn't freeze things – ice-cream, for instance! We can also have peas and beans all the year round and not just in summer.

Living in the Arctic is like living in a fridge

In the sides of a refrigerator or freezer are pipes that contain a special, cold fluid. This cold fluid is pumped through the pipes to carry heat away from the food in the refrigerator and keep it cold. As it goes through the pipes it changes from a **liquid** to a **vapour** – this makes the vapour take up a lot of heat. The food is then kept cold! If you put your hand behind a fridge you can feel the warm air coming out.

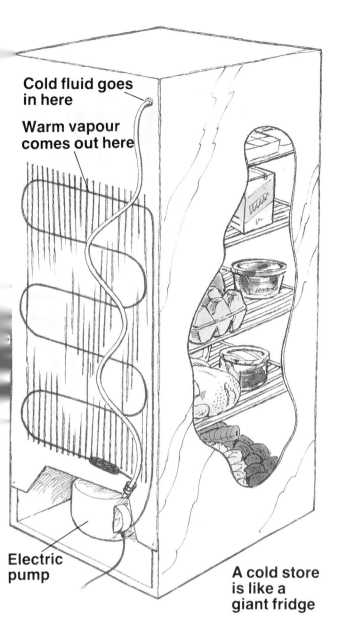

Cold fluid goes
in here

Warm vapour
comes out here

Electric
pump

A cold store
is like a
giant fridge

Freezing Facts

Have you heard of Birdseye, the famous frozen food company? It was named after the American Clarence Birdseye. He was on a trading expedition to Labrador in 1916 and was fascinated by the way Inuit stored seal meat for months in deep wells in the ice. When he got home he tried to recreate the same method of preserving food. Eight years later he had found the way which is still used today.

There are some very juicy foods that are very difficult to freeze because they have a lot of water in them, like strawberries, melons and oranges. Although they freeze easily, when they defrost the ice flows away as water and takes all the taste with it! Some foods have to be blanched before they are frozen. This means they are dipped briefly in boiling water, to kill any **impurities** in them.

In the kitchen today

There are several different ways of cooking the same food, which alters its taste. If you have some bread and an egg you could make an egg sandwich, but just think what else you could do with them.

You can *boil* the egg in its shell in water. If you put the bread under the *grill* on the cooker you can have toast fingers with it. You might prefer to *fry* both the egg and the bread in some oil in the frying pan. Or maybe scramble the egg and serve it on buttered toast.

Electric toasters now give you slice after slice of toast which pops up when it is cooked so that you don't have to watch the toast all the time to see if it's burning.

Non-stick pans are coated with something that scientists developed during the space programme that means you will not leave half your fried egg stuck to the bottom of the pan.

If you want to give a different flavour or **texture** to your food then you could put some in an electric mixer or blender to change the texture or add different ingredients to change the flavour.

Nowadays you may have a **thermostat** on your cooker to keep the heat exactly right, and an electric timer you can set to tell you when it is ready. In the past people roasted their dinner over an open fire. Sometimes they put the meat on a **spit** before the fire and turned it to cook the meat evenly. Sometimes they used a dog running in a wheel to turn the spit.

Cooking over a fire

Spit-roasting

Victorian cooker

Modern cooker

A new wave

Have you ever been to a café or restaurant and had to wait for ages to get the food you ordered? If you are in a hurry or very hungry it can make you very cross. Now thanks to an American invention of 1947 that is all changing. An entirely new way of cooking using a microwave cooker is found in many restaurants, and homes as well. Cooking this way is very fast – sometimes taking only a few seconds. Compare the cooking instructions on the packet of a frozen meat pie – about 30 minutes in a normal oven, compared with 4 minutes in a microwave cooker.

We are used to seeing quite large ovens in our kitchens, and waiting even hours for our food to cook in them. A microwave cooker is much smaller as well as quicker because it does not have burning flames or red-hot plates like gas and electric cookers. Inside the little box invisible heat rays bombard the food. Though we can't see them they heat the food like the sun's rays heat us. Microwaves **penetrate** into the food so it cooks on the inside at the same time as the outside. That is why it is so much quicker! You have to be careful to use only dishes made from glass, china or plastic in these ovens, metal dishes make the rays bounce off and the food doesn't cook!

Microwave oven

Some people do not like microwave ovens because they think food should cook slowly and thoroughly and also food does not go brown when cooked by microwaves. This can put people off. Others are worried about using **radiation**.

Most people are getting used to the idea of microwaved food because it is so quick and easy

The bread on your plate

BEGIN HERE

Bread has been an important food for thousands of years. The Ancient Greeks grew wheat to make bread, just as we do today. In a museum in Italy there is a 1900-year-old loaf! It came out of a sealed oven at Pompeii. Often, if people were poor they didn't eat much else. In 1845 a farm labourer spent 12p a week on rent and 14p on bread for his family! We still eat a lot of bread today. You are going to find out how to make, and experiment with, bread.

First of all, look at these two pages. Try reading **Look Around** and the poem. On the next page there are some investigations for you to try. Finding out about something is called research. You are doing research into bread. Try to make notes about your research while you are doing it. It helps you to remember later on.

The boy stood in the supper-room

The boy stood in the supper-room
   Whence all but he had fled;
He'd eaten several pots of jam
   And he was gorged with bread.

'Oh, one more crust before I bust!!'
   He cried in accents wild
He licked the plates, he sucked the
   spoons –
   He was a vulgar child.

There came a burst of thunder-sound
   The boy – oh! where was he?
Ask of the maid who mopped him up,
   The bread crumbs and the tea!

Anonymous

Look around

Go and look at the shelves of bread and buns at the baker's shop or supermarket. Bread comes in many shapes, sizes and even colours. How many different sorts can you find? If some of you have packaged bread at home perhaps you could compare the lists of ingredients that are printed on the wrapping paper. Look at how different they are. Remember, ingredients are printed in order of quantity. That means that whatever ingredient there is most of in bread will come first in the list. Is there anything in bread that you are surprised to see there? What is wheatgerm? Is brown bread really better for you than white? What is the difference between white and brown bread?

Places

Baker's shop
Canning factory
Dairy
Farms – dairy and arable
Local environmental
    health office
Local shops &
    supermarkets
Local history museum

Books

The Making of Food, Paul Nash, Young Library 1984
Tomorrow's World – Food, van den Brul & Spindler, BBC
The Pooh Cook Book, Katie Stewart, Methuen
Waste Not, Want Not – Food, Anne-Marie Constant, Burke
Bread, P.B. Roscoe, Ladybird Leaders
Children's Britannica, *under* Bread and Food

Words

You will come across some unusual words in your investigations. If you do not know the meaning of a word you could try the word list on page 31 of this book, or use a dictionary. Here are some of the words you may need to look up:

ingredients   recipe
knead   tepid

Bread recipe

To make your own bread you will need quite a lot of time, and quite strong muscles! Remember to keep your hands clean at all times! This is an old method that people have used for centuries.

Ingredients

1 kg (2 lb) strong plain flour
570 ml (19 fl oz) tepid water
3 level teaspoons salt
30 g (1 oz) fresh yeast or 4 teaspoons dried yeast
1 level teaspoon sugar

Put the flour and salt into a warm bowl. Stir the yeast and sugar together in another bowl with some of the water. Make a little hollow in the middle of the flour and put the yeast mixture into it. Sprinkle some flour on top of it, put a cloth over the bowl and leave for about 15 minutes. Now add the rest of the water and mix it all together.

Knead well until the dough is smooth and does not stick to the bowl, about five minutes.

Leave the dough to rise in a warm place (like an airing cupboard) for about an hour and a half – then knead well again.

Leave the dough to rise again for another hour.

Sprinkle some flour onto a board and put the dough on it and knead again!

Cut the dough into rolls – or put it into greased tins (at least half full)

Leave for another 20 minutes before putting it into a hot oven. Be very careful! The oven should be set at 400F, 200C, Gas mark 6 for the first ten minutes and then at 350F, 180C, Gas mark 4 for 30 to 45 minutes – until they are cooked. The rolls will take less time than the bread.

Keep it

Some of the bread you buy has preservatives in it. Some people like to buy bread with no additives at all in it – like the bread you have made. Put a slice of your bread, one from an additive-free loaf and one or two from loaves with preservatives onto plates and leave them on a shelf for a few days. Look at them every day. Which slices go mouldy first?

Colour up

When you are making your bread, try adding some food colouring during the final kneading to bits of the dough and cooking them into rolls…blue rolls, green rolls, red rolls. Try to use additive-free colouring. You will only need a tiny drop. Get your friends to taste the rolls – they may say they can tell the difference. Now do a blindfold test. Can they taste which one is blue without looking?

TAKE IT FROM HERE

Maybe you could try cooking other foods now, and make a book of the recipes you use. Try writing a story or poem about your favourite food or find some in other books.

Things you need

2 large bowls
scales
measuring jug
cloth
board
teaspoon
wooden spoons
bread tins OR
baking sheets
food colourings